EYE TO EYE
HEART TO HEART

A Reflection on Wycliffe Bible Translators and Vision 2025

Wycliffe Bible Translators

Published by Wycliffe Bible Translators of Canada Inc.,
4316 10 St NE, Calgary, AB T2E 6K3 Canada

ISBN 978-0-9680135-1-9

Text by Dave and Deborah Crough
Photographs by Dave Crough
Text editing by Dwayne Janke
Design by Laird Salkeld

Printed in Canada by McCallum Printing Group Inc., Edmonton, Alberta, Canada

Cover: Cambodia, 2001. **Previous page:** Bolivia, 2005. **Back cover:** West Asia, 1997.

Wycliffe Bible Translators has a worldwide presence. The umbrella organization, Wycliffe International, gives coordinating oversight to an association of member organizations bound together by the desire to see the Word of God translated into every language that needs it. Because Wycliffe and affiliated organizations believe Bible translation is part of the Great Commission's mandate to the Church, they actively seek to engage the worldwide Church in the Bible translation ministry. These organizations partner with churches and other mission agencies in their countries to present Bible translation to the Christian public in order to raise resources—funds, prayer and personnel—for the cause.

Partners in Bible Translation

Partners in Bible Translation

Wycliffe Bible Translators
P.O. Box 628200
Orlando, FL 32862
www.wycliffe.org
info_usa@wycliffe.org
1-800-992-5433

Wycliffe Bible Translators of Canada
4316 10 St NE
Calgary AB T2E 6K3
www.wycliffe.ca
info@wycliffe.ca
1-800-463-1143

For additional copies of this book, contact:

(in the U.S.)
www.wycliffe.org/shop.aspx
mrco@wycliffe.org
1-800-992-5433, ext. 3778

(in Canada)
www.wycliffe.ca/store
media_resources@wycliffe.ca
1-800-463-1143, ext. 283

For more information about becoming involved with Wycliffe and *Vision 2025* in countries around the world, contact:

www.wycliffe.net

Dedication

Canada, 1999. Bob and Ruth Chapman.

Observing a life in motion is like watching a film—we know the parts we've already seen, but not what is to come. An earthly life completed is more like a photograph. It holds still, allowing us to examine, to consider, to contemplate each detail, and to adopt meaning for our own lives.

On January 30, 2000, when a Kenya Airways Airbus fell into the ocean off the Ivory Coast in West Africa, Wycliffe missionaries Bob and Ruth Chapman rose heavenward to join their sons Ross and Timothy, who died in 1989 from cerebral malaria. Their daughter Erin was living in Canada at the time of her parents' death.

With Erin's blessing, we lovingly dedicate this book to Bob and Ruth.

Jesus said, "By this all will know that you are my disciples, if you have love for one another" (John 13:35 NKJV). It wouldn't be possible to count the hearts of those all around the world that have been touched in some profound way by the Chapmans. Their devotion to God and family; their work for Bibleless people groups in Africa through their leadership roles in Cameroon and later, throughout Africa; their home continually open and their time available to colleagues and Cameroonian neighbors alike; Bob's outreach to Cameroonians in prison; Ruth's myriad friendships where she counseled, comforted and encouraged; Bob's incredible sense of humor and Ruth's gentle, sweet voice—all have left indelible marks wherever the two went.

Had they known the number of their days, it seems unlikely they could have lived their lives any more effectively, nor left a better image in our minds and hearts of what the love of God looks like. It's as if they could see beyond this present life, with its many joys and sorrows, to focus on the greater joy to come.

Bob and Ruth have received their promised reward. They comprehend the full picture now—with an eternal perspective.

"For now we see through a glass, darkly; but then face to face: now I know in part; but then shall I know even as also I am known" (1 Corinthians 13:12 KJV).

Foreword

Vision 2025—Serving in partnership worldwide to see
Bible translation begun by 2025 in every remaining
language community that needs it.

As we move deeper into the 21st century, we see God's Word impacting lives across the globe. The growth of His Church is significant proof that He is alive and at work, and that His Word is active in the hearts and minds of people of all cultures. It's amazing to realize that God chooses to communicate through people's heart languages. He is not limited to English, French or Mandarin; nor does God require that His Word be available only in the original biblical languages of Hebrew, Aramaic or Greek.

Translating God's message into the languages of the world has been an important part of spreading the gospel. Ever since the first translation—that of the Hebrew Old Testament into Greek, 2,300 years ago—God has blessed the efforts of those who've made Bible translation a priority. Church history shows a clear link between the translation of the Scriptures, a response to the gospel, and the endurance of Christianity over many generations.

I know firsthand the impact the Word of God can have on a group of people. I grew up in a small community in the mountains of Papua New Guinea, where my parents helped the West Kewa people have the Scriptures in their own language. The New Testament translation was completed in 1973, and has since been revised and reprinted. A group of West Kewa translators—the fruit of having the New Testament—is working on the Old Testament. One day the growing West Kewa church will have the whole Bible to guide their lives and community.

Because of my personal experience, the content of the book you are holding is deeply meaningful to me. This book reflects photographically what God is doing with people on the margins of the world, people like those with whom I grew up. As long as I can remember I've loved photographs, especially photos that show people in their surroundings, living life, enjoying the good in their culture, celebrating family and worshipping God. I believe good

photojournalism draws its viewer into the heart of its subjects. It does so by capturing their moods, the nuances of their expressions and feelings. It preserves these for the viewer to look at, study, be moved by. A photo-based book such as this one leads the viewer from the role of observer to that of participant—one involved in life, in the creativity and diversity of God's creation, and ultimately in worship of God, the very creator and giver of all life.

This book's photographer-authors are friends of mine, and I greatly respect their talent and their desire to use it for the cause of Christ. Through their work, we're taken across the world's time zones to see for ourselves evidence that the Holy Spirit is actively stirring up a movement. It's a movement used by the Lord to permeate nations by crossing cultural, social, economic, political and linguistic barriers. The Word of God speaks for itself in all human situations because it's translatable into every language.

This book also reveals the context and progress towards *Vision 2025*. This vision is not yet fulfilled; there is an enormous need for greater awareness and participation. It is a vital part of the work of the Church worldwide. For *Vision 2025* to be realized, substantially more people must participate. Increases in prayer support and funding for every language project are also critical for the vision to be achieved.

Each of the world's language groups represents men, women, children, families and communities who will someday face God. They need His Word in a language they can understand so they can meet Him now and truly know His heart. May God use this book to give you a heart for ever greater involvement in this vision to make mother tongue Scripture available where it is still needed, by those who still need Him.

—Kirk Franklin, Executive Director, Wycliffe International

Introduction:
From John Wycliffe to Vision 2025

How the insight of a man from the 14th century still guides his namesake's mission organization in the 21st century.

The only thing you will find in a grave is what is decomposing. Except for one notable and gloriously empty tomb, re-excavation unearths only bones.

But in 1415, so great was the anger and indignation of the Church hierarchy toward priest and scholar John Wycliffe, that the Council of Constance declared him a heretic—30 years after his death on December 31, 1384. Condemning him on 267 counts, this gathering of Catholic bishops from all parts of Europe ordered that Wycliffe's writings be burned and his bones be exhumed from his grave. For good measure, he was excommunicated.

Wycliffe's crime, which provoked such severe action, was that he declared it the right of all people of every class to be able to read the Bible in their mother tongue. "Christ and His Apostles taught the people in the language best known to them," he observed. "Believers should have the Scriptures in a language which they fully understand." With this conviction, in the final four years of his life, Wycliffe oversaw the first translation of the Bible into the English language.

It took another 13 years after the Council's declaration for the Church to execute the defaming order against Wycliffe. To make things final, his bones were burned and the ashes scattered.

The act backfired.

As English churchman and historian Thomas Fuller strikingly pointed out:

"They burnt his bones to ashes and cast them into the Swift, a neighboring brook, running hard by. Thus the brook hath conveyed his ashes into Avon; Avon into Severn; Severn into the narrow seas; and they into the main ocean. And thus the ashes of Wycliffe are the emblem of his doctrine which now is dispersed the world over."

The impact of Wycliffe's thinking spread, washing over the whole world. Declared to be the "Morningstar of the Reformation," Wycliffe's influence continued to flow through the lives of William Tyndale, John Huss, Martin Luther, William Carey and many others. Eventually, near the beginning of the 20th century, it filled the heart and mind of a young man named Cameron Townsend, and another, John Watters, on the threshold of the 21st century.

A memorial located in St. Mary's Church, Lutterworth, England, depicts John Wycliffe preaching to villagers. The inscription reads in part: "His labours in the cause of Scriptural truth were crowned by one immortal achievement; his translation of the Bible into the English tongue. . . . He found an abundant reward in the blessing of his countrymen, of every rank and age, to whom he unfolded the words of eternal life."

Quebec, Canada, 1998. Translator Cécile Mapachee holds her copy of the Algonquin New Testament.

Cameroon, 2003. The Baka people are one of several Pygmy groups living across Central Africa. The Baka language is complex, and is known as a linguistic isolate—yet its continued usage is a key to the cultural and spiritual survival of its speakers, like this boy.

Dallas, U.S.A., 2002. Peter Martin inspects some of his handiwork. He creates digital forms of writing systems for translating and publishing Scripture in languages that don't use the Roman alphabet.

New York City, U.S.A., 1999. Alan MacDonald, at the United Nations headquarters, works the phone in building relationships with ambassadors and government officials. He carries on the longstanding imperative of being of service to all as voiced by Wycliffe's founder, Cameron Townsend.

Wycliffe's vision reaches a new horizon

A vision without a task is a dream.
A task without a vision is drudgery.
A vision with a task is the hope of the world.

— Anonymous

While selling Spanish Bibles in Guatemala in 1917, Cameron Townsend discovered that the Cakchiquel Indians he met couldn't speak or read Spanish. He abandoned his job in order to live among the Cakchiquel and learn their language. It turned out to be a very difficult undertaking. For example, a single Cakchiquel verb can take thousands of possible forms. However, in a remarkable 10 years' time, Townsend had indeed learned the language, created an alphabet, analyzed the grammar and translated the New Testament. His own vision was forming as he worked out the blueprint for what would later become Wycliffe Bible Translators, a key partner in the now rapidly expanding worldwide Bible translation movement.

It started in 1934, as Townsend introduced two students to his translation program at what he called Camp Wycliffe, named in honor of John Wycliffe. It later became known as the Summer Institute of Linguistics, since classes were then held only in the summer.

When Townsend took up the cause of minority language groups in Central and South America, missions work done using dominant languages was the standard approach of the day; minority language communities were expected to assimilate. However, in time, Townsend's peripheral vision of working in the mother tongue became the prevailing view. Also, his commitment to serve and relate to all (including governments and the surrounding secular society) with love and respect, was largely unprecedented in mission efforts at the time.

Today there are more than 60 Wycliffe and affiliated organizations around the world, operating as a confederation of mission agencies to promote, support and engage in Bible translation.

The umbrella organization, Wycliffe International, gives coordinating oversight.

Same goal, new roadmap

"A vision . . . provides a destination from which we can derive a roadmap, so we know the direction we should take."

—Dr. John Watters

Visionaries very often don't live to see the fulfillment of their idea, or at least not all it will accomplish. They are usually far ahead of the people and structure needed to bring their vision to completion. Sometimes when results begin to materialize, another person reinterprets the concept, and catapults it ahead to a new horizon.

In 1999 Dr. John Watters, the incoming executive director of Wycliffe International and an experienced translator himself, was struck by an alarming realization: if new Bible translation projects continued to be started at the same rate, the world's languages would not all receive God's Word until, at best, 2150. Convinced this was unacceptable, Watters imparted compelling reasons to accelerate the pace of vernacular Scripture translation, and proposed various paradigm shifting strategies to do so. He called this *Vision 2025*, and it has become the roadmap for the Wycliffe family of organizations. The core goal of *Vision 2025* is:

"Serving in partnership worldwide to see Bible translation begun by 2025 in every remaining language community that needs it."

Vision 2025 stands on five pillars or themes:

Urgency: This has more to do with recognizing and responding to the great need, than to adopting a hurried pace. Emphasis is on service to all, especially those who have been denied access to God's Word. Realizing that people from every tribe, tongue and nation will appear before the throne of God, they are to be treated with fairness, respect and honor.

Papua New Guinea, 1990. Here, as in other countries, the efforts of vernacular translation manifest themselves in far-reaching applications. Children—and adults—learn best in their own language, before then bridging into a national language. Thus, mother tongue literacy programs are highly important in the overall work of Wycliffe and its partners.

Peru, 2005. Justin Hettinga presents newly published booklets to Cusco Quechua-speaking women. The booklets, written in their language by other Quechua, use Scriptural principles to address common social issues that are relevant to these women.

West Asia, 1997. Cross-cultural acclimation is important to fitting in and building relationships.

Mali, 2004. Pastor Ibrahim Ag Mohamed, here with his Polish wife Gosia and their daughter, was the guiding force behind the Tamasheq Scripture translation project. The Tamasheq are mainly nomadic desert dwellers of the Sahara, but have settlements in towns like Timbuktu. Pastor Ibrahim observed, "Even we who are believers are only pilgrims on this earth. We are called to settle one day in eternity, so we will not be just wanderers."

Partnership: This acknowledges that more can be done better by working with others than can be achieved by one's own efforts. There is more openness today to cooperation and partnerships between churches, mission organizations and individuals than ever before.

Capacity Building: This involves assisting language communities and partners to develop the necessary skills, expertise, infrastructure and network of relations to undertake language development and Bible translation projects. Today the non-Western Church outnumbers the Western Church by more than three to one. There is an increasing need to invite and engage others to serve in the ministry of Bible translation, and to invest in their lives through training, mentoring and consulting.

Creative Strategies: The need to multiply efforts requires experimenting with new ideas and strategies in training, partnering and new technology. It's important to remember that partners may share a common goal of people and communities transformed by God's Word, but have different ways of achieving it. Partners can be unified in spirit, but not uniform in action; have similar motivation, but use different working styles and have radically different cultural assumptions.

Sustainability: The goal is to invest in people and processes by which they can maintain their own language and translation programs. As language communities gain the capacity to continue by themselves, outside involvement should diminish.

After the first six years of its implementation, the effect of *Vision 2025's* cooperative strategies, as employed by an ever increasing number of partners worldwide, reduced the timeline of starting Bible translation projects by over 110 years. And yet, more than 2,000 of the world's nearly 7,000 languages are still without God's Word. Clearly, working harder is not the answer. Thinking differently, being open to change, while still heading toward the original goal—that is a journey with a purpose that unites the Wycliffe family.

This book, illustrated photographically, presents reflections on *Vision 2025*, as it relates personally to those involved in numerous aspects of the translation process.

God: The first translator

Perhaps more important than anything else, Bible translation allows people to hear directly from God. John Wycliffe held each person's right to this knowledge as his deepest, most personal belief. His actions, and the actions of those who have followed his footsteps, aim pointedly in the direction of individual freedom and dignity, through an understanding of the Creator.

The ultimate translation project occurred when God's Word became incarnate in Jesus. God Himself was translated into human form, so that we could know Him personally. Ultimately, the vision we are striving to fulfill, the task at hand, is not of our making, but His. It's His heart calling out to our hearts, to all hearts, until that day when we all see Him eye to eye.

—Deborah Crough, Calgary, Canada, Summer 2007

Eye has not seen, nor ear heard,
Nor have entered into the heart of man
The things which God has prepared for those who love Him.
—1 Corinthians 2:9 (NKJV)

Contents

*You are our epistle written in our hearts, known and read by all
. . . written not with ink but by the Spirit of the living God, not
on tablets of stone but on tablets of flesh, that is, of the heart.*
—2 Corinthians 3:2,3 (NKJV)

West
Asia,
1997.

Mali,
2004.

The best time to plant a tree was 20 years ago.
The second best time is today.
—Chinese proverb

I made the photographs presented in this book over the past 20 years. The time finally seemed right to "plant" them in a book. Some have been reproduced in various Wycliffe publications. But it was not until contemplating aspects of *Vision 2025* that I got the idea of bringing together images to reflect upon its many facets.

As a missionary staff member of Wycliffe Bible Translators, it's been a major part of my assignment to visit colleagues and partners all over the world. I have had the privilege of helping to present co-workers' stories as they play out in the worldwide Bible translation movement. It dawned on me that what I'd so often encountered on these trips were examples of all the themes of *Vision 2025*—even though prior to 1999, no one had given a name to them.

The challenge of this book became editing together photographs taken over the years into a meaningful context. I took a lesson from my linguist/translator colleagues. They often employ what's known as dynamic equivalence, or meaning-based translation principles, when referencing source biblical texts, to determine how best to translate original meanings into the vernacular language(s) in which they're working. The goal is a translation that speaks truthfully and easily to native speakers—a translation that local communities can embrace. This book aims to present a visually dynamic, meaning-based "translation" of *Vision 2025*—in a manner people can embrace.

The opening page of each of the five *Vision 2025* theme sections that follow presents a treatment of these themes. The text of each includes references from source documents chiefly composed by Dr. John Watters, executive director of Wycliffe International, 2000-2007.

In a book project of this nature, it is impossible to portray the entire depth and breadth of the efforts of the thousands who are, and have been, so vitally and sacrificially involved in Bible translation and other language-related ministries, including those who serve in supporting these efforts. This book presents an overview of the variety of ways that people relate in service to others, so people groups without mother tongue Scripture can ultimately understand God's Word—and be transformed by it.

Naturally, this Christian motivation is not shared or appreciated by some in various locations where our colleagues and partners work. Thus, occasionally only vague identifying factors will be found in some photo captions. Additionally, people's roles that are mentioned in captions were accurate at the times noted in the captions.

Toward the end of the book, there is a section that, at first glance, seems to stray from the overall concept of *Vision 2025*. It is a photo essay on the Waorani of Ecuador, and is included for two reasons: 1) the ability to devote more page space to a single people group serves to illustrate the holistic nature of service to, and learning from, a language community, and 2) the Waorani story, which is ongoing, is arguably one of the most central and influential in terms of cross-cultural missions in the 20th century—and presents a people group transformed by God's Word. That impact has integrity which stands in any time period, under any missionary banner. Special appreciation is given to anthropologist Dr. James Yost for source documents from which text was derived in this section.

Finally, there is a section on prayer, where it simply seemed best to let the images and Scripture speak their own stories.

PREFACE · · · PREFACE · · · PREFACE · · · PREFACE · · · PREFACE · · · PREFACE · · · PREFACE · · · PREFACE · · · PREFACE

In 1989, I had flown and motor-canoed to a remote village location in Papua New Guinea along the Sepik River. As I was photographing among the villagers, an old man put his hand on my shoulder and thanked me for coming to visit. Then he rocketed out of his mouth a quantity of betel nut juice. I then took a picture of him doing it again. To this day, I really don't know which act is stranger: the spitting or taking a photo of it. But I do know one thing—like the saying that no snowflake ever falls in the wrong place, no photograph is *not* meant to be.

—Dave Crough, Calgary, Canada, Summer 2007

Mali, 2004.

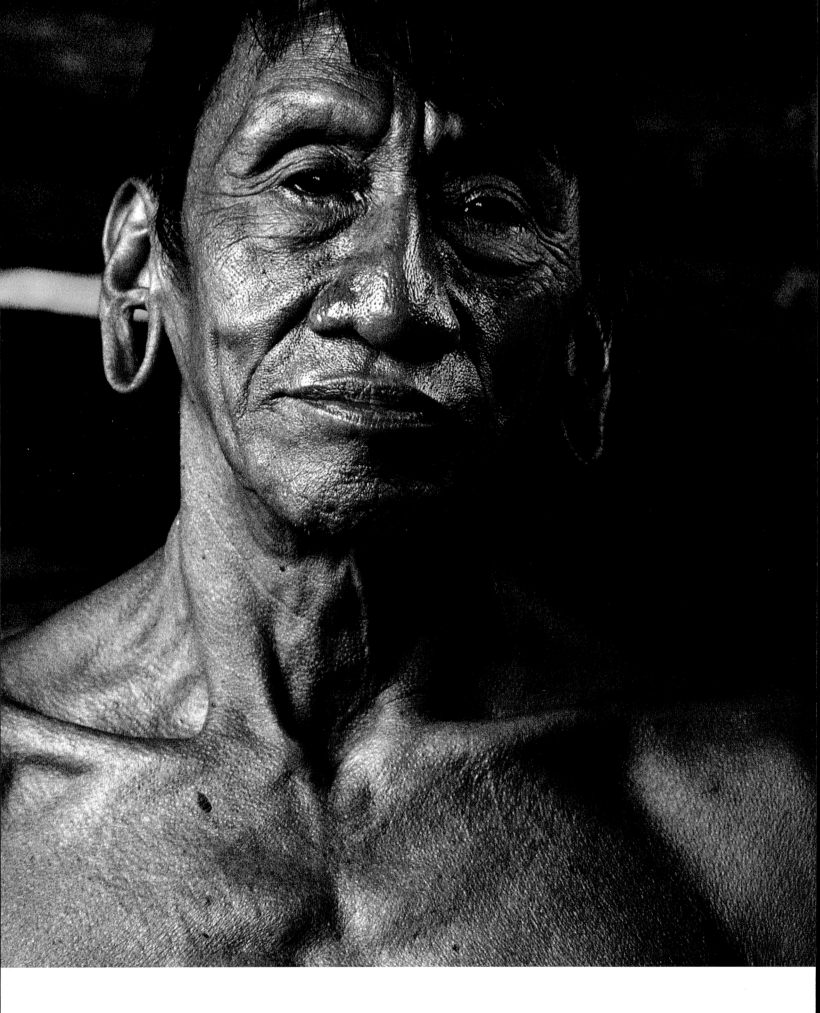

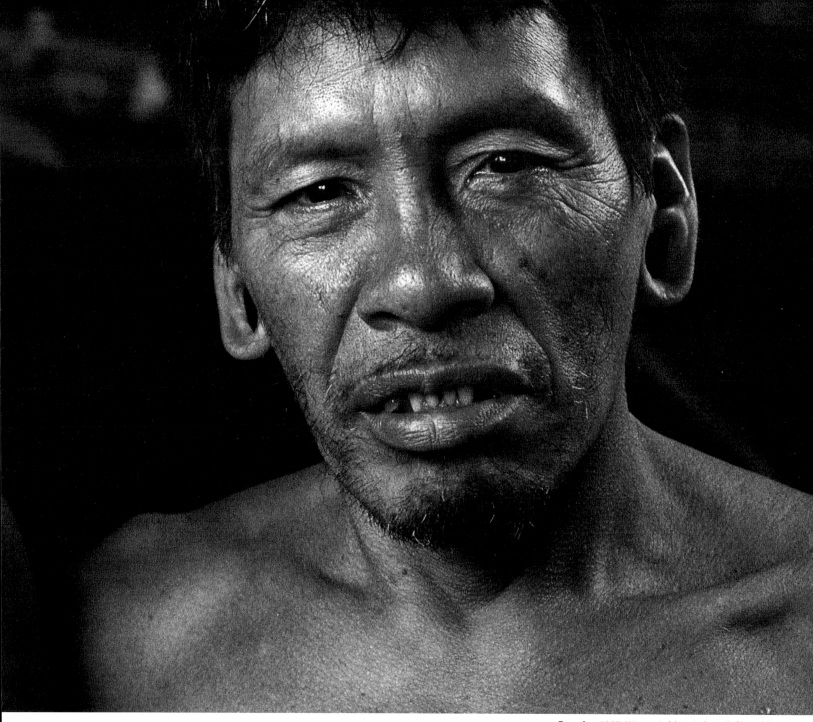

Ecuador, 1987. Waorani elders Geketa (left) and Dewey, two of the Palm Beach killers from 1956. (See pg. 120.)

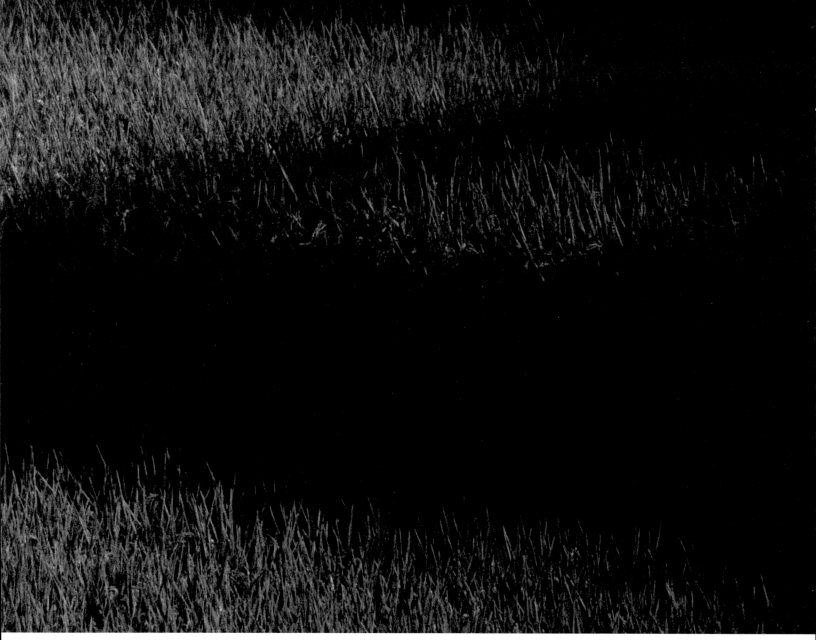

East Asia, 1998.

Urgency It's About Purpose

For the worldwide family of Christian mission agencies known as Wycliffe Bible Translators, along with numerous partnering organizations, our sense of urgency is based on God's deep affection for humanity. He desires that individuals from every tribe, language, people and nation on earth enter into an eternal relationship with Him. This perception of urgency, as it relates to *Vision 2025*, energizes and emboldens us to make the Word of God accessible to the language communities of the earth sooner rather than later. Yet it focuses more on intention than on haste or speed.

It often appears that at no time is there enough time for all we feel we need to do with the time we're given. But appearances can be deceiving. How can we make better use of our time? As we serve God and help fulfill His desire, we seek to be good stewards of the resources He has given us. We do this by discovering, developing and strengthening the ability in others; by being innovative and resourceful in the way we work; and by always aiming to leave behind translation and other language-related ministries that will outlive our presence.

To achieve these objectives raises issues of how we might work differently rather than harder, and so meet the needs of language communities without Scripture in their mother tongues. Urgency motivates us to be more inclusive as to who leads language projects and with whom we might partner. We must consider additional creative means to guide us in allocating our human and financial resources more effectively. Urgency in our personal and corporate lives involves much diligent, earnest, resolute, insistent, firm, purposeful effort.

An urgent and ongoing awareness of one's purpose in relation to God—that's a vision that breeds lasting contentment.

Therefore, my beloved brethren, be steadfast, immovable, always abounding in the work of the Lord, knowing that your labor is not in vain in the Lord.

—1 Corinthians 15:58 (NKJV)

India,
2006

Northwest Territories, Canada, 2002. Dogrib elder, Elizabeth MacKenzie, is a resolute inspiration to her daughter, Mary, a main mother tongue translator for the Dogrib New Testament. Elizabeth, eyes dimmed by diabetes, said, "If we understand God's Word in our language, the world becomes small. It's like holding the world. Everything seems to come together." I've come to understand that she sees more than what this photograph reveals.

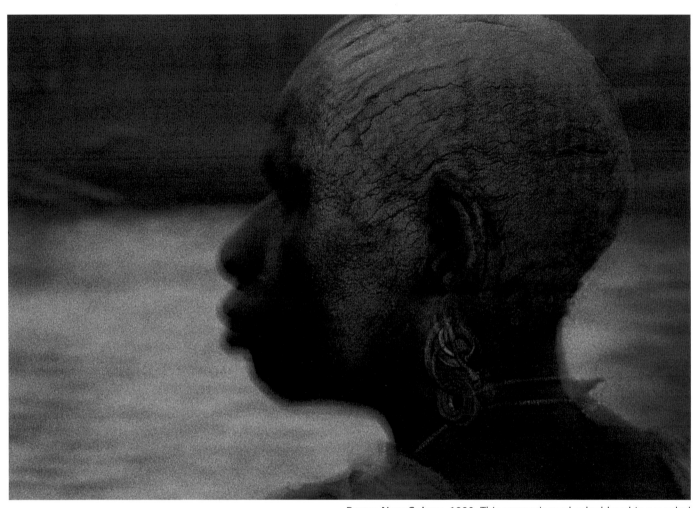

Papua New Guinea, 1990. This woman's mud-caked head is a symbol of mourning. With more than 800 languages in the small island nation, Papua New Guinea (PNG) has provided numerous examples of how expatriate Wycliffe personnel and PNG's Christians have come to work together. This is not always easy, and speaks to the notion in *Vision 2025* of allowing for cross-cultural differences in partnerships. Our family lived in PNG for a little over a year (our daughter was born there). In our support roles as writer and photographer, respectively, my wife Deb and I trained Papua New Guinean colleagues in our areas of expertise. It seemed only natural—especially among new friends.

East Asia, 1998. A translator at his desk. It takes a will to carry on. A sacrifice of self. A voluntary submission. Learning these precepts personally is perhaps, from God's perspective, the most urgent need of all—and a prerequisite of encouraging these attributes in others.

[1] Paul, Silase mbɔɔ Timothée, naa yɔɔn ŋwa'ne mbwo cu'te pʉa Kristo a gie aa

Thessalonica ngwɔ́ cu'te pʉa Tá wege Sse, mbɔɔ ye Cʉapʉa wege Yěso Kristo. [2] Á poŋ ngie

E Sse Ta m

Sse Tá mbɔɔ Cʉapʉa wege Yěso Kristo neŋ mbʉle na pi, ńgiŋe ntsɔɔn meziŋe mi.

Cʉapʉa yěsó kristo ne ngwɔ̃ ne ʌi ʉne neŋe sʉ̈ʉ̈te ntʉʉ̈m pí

Letsɔ'te metsaŋ gẅie me zăb ntii lyɛ' gie Yěso Kristo gé tó

Cʉapʉa ge gyo tó ɲag pʉa mesɔŋ

[3] Mefɛ mefɛ, peg gẅiin lesẅiŋte Sse na two sí ngwoŋ fʉ' ntseŋ, mela'mie pi te ně nkʉa

lena ndǎg mbwo Sse na two sí *fʉ̈ mbɔŋ ngie peg gyo pʉʉ*

lezab ntʉm na yé wɔ́, ńgiŋe ne ngẅiin nkwoŋe tsetsɛ pi metsem. [4] Á cʉa pú'ú tá peg waa

ʌdsɔɔ ngee pʌ le ʉɛo

nkím leziŋ si tsɛ metsɔ́ menda cu'te pʉa Sse, ntʉm weg ne nkaga kǎg mela'mie pʉa ne nnyɛɛ

me *nkɪm pʌ ne ka'te*

gẅi nguŋgʉ, ńně nkʉe gẅi pi ke te cu'te kyo, pi ke shʉɔg shʉɔg ne nzaba ntʉm gẅi pɔ na

ʌně

Yěso Kristo. Yě zɔ̌ mbwo peg ngwɔ́ no ka'te ntii gẅi. [5] Yɔɔn lɔgɔ nnyɛɛ ngie Sse ge la' lɔg

A *e Sse ɲag ntsa*

pɔ no nenʉ ŋag pʉa pa' pi gya ngɔ' pɛ'ɛ lè. Á lɔgɔ nyɛɛ ngie pi ku'u leku tsɛ lefuɔ Sse sie pi

nʉltʉ nʉltʉ . Anʉɛ ngʌsʌ gie pi ne ngya fʉʌɔn, e gyo ngie ʌi kʋʌ pʉa pie pi

gya ngɔ' ntii sě. [6] Pi zse mbɔnɔ ngie Sse ge lá' ŋag ntsaŋ pɔ pa'a ne nzɛte, é na ngɔ' mbwo

sš lefuɔ Sse. Pi gya ngʌ́ ntii pʌ pʉʌ

pʉa pie nnyɛ gẅi ngɔ' fʉ'ɔɔn lɔɔn. [7] A ge la' naa sẅete mbwo pi pie pi ne ngya ngɔ' fʉ'ɔɔn

pie e nyɛ̈ *e*

ʌɔn, é giŋe nna mbɔɔ mbwo peg yeg, Cʉapʉa wege Yěso a fó tyo lepwo ngwâ sẅe' mecʉɔ'

Mɔɔn me no ye la' cʉʌte afʉ'gie Cʉapʉa wege yěsó ge

tyo lepwo e kʉ̈ɛ, nyɛ mbʉm ye, pa̋ me cp̌' pe pie e glʉ̈iin n

Cameroon, 2003. Here's an example of why one needs to start sooner rather than later. This is a draft page from a translation of 2 Thessalonians in the Ngiemboon language. The notations from a consultant identify sections where unnatural grammatical structures were used—and need to be fixed. Ouch.

Peru, 2005. Marcelina Huamán was once entangled with the Maoist terrorist group, *Shining Path.* She has only become literate in her native Cusco Quechua language in the past decade, and now pastors and plants churches, like the one seen here, in small Quechua communities. *Vision 2025* is not just about producing vernacular Scriptures at a faster pace. It's ultimately about transformed lives. It's about Marcelina.

East Asia, 1998 (both). (Left) A young mother walks her son to a local school (above), where he and his sister are the only foreigners. Besides language learning, besides cross-cultural adaptation, besides struggling with the need to let go of her child's hand, she writes poetry (**see below and opposite**). There is always time for art in the midst of the urgent.

So Much To Do in So Little Time

The days speed quickly by
The time is getting nearer
But the Lord our God
Is a God who makes things clearer.

The pressure's mounting high
The time is getting shorter
But the Lord our God
Is a God of perfect order.

There's still so much to do
The time is getting hurried
But the Lord our God
Is a God who doesn't get worried.

West Asia, 1997 (both). Where will the children play? Where they feel at home. And where is home? Where they are loved and cared for—where Mom and Dad are. The power in all our plans to minister among minority people groups pales in comparison with the simple trust of a child.

Don't Drink the Water in the Bottom of the Cup
Mama always told me to drink it all up.
Mama always told me don't leave a drop in the cup.
Mama always told me to do what I was told,
But Mama's never been over here.

India, 2006. Unlike many children from tribal communities across India, this girl (observing an adult mother tongue literacy class) can look forward to both an educational and spiritual foundation—in her own language, Halbi. That's due in no small part to rapidly expanding efforts of one of the newest Wycliffe member organizations: Word For All, in India.

Montreal, Canada, 1998. Don and Thelma Webster had several careers within Wycliffe before they moved into a pastoral ministry in a multi-ethnic church in Montreal. Their story ranges from a translation project among the Inupiat in Alaska (during which time their firstborn child died), to helping start up Wycliffe's work in two African countries—no instruction manual included. Having visited and photographed numerous people groups worldwide where reverence and respect for community elders is paramount, I've observed that *taking the time* to confer first with your elders most often *speeds up* any agenda one might have.

Papua New Guinea, 1990. The Ama people in East Sepik Province numbered 400 when I visited during a ceremony dedicating the New Testament in their language. Are some language groups too small to warrant the allocation of limited resources? Before forming an answer, look at the boy in the foreground holding the leaf. Look at his eyes.

Yellowknife, Canada, 2002. The first-draft print-out of the typeset New Testament in the Dogrib language. That day, the Dogrib translation team did some final checking—but one woman, after thumbing through it, remarked, "This is a *real* treaty. This one will never change."

Mali, 2004. The place where Christians are buried in Timbuktu. So many before us have sacrificed so much—and lived faithfully, unbent by opposition. A summation of this is beautifully described in a passage from George Eliot's book, *Middlemarch*: ". . . for the growing good of the world is partly dependent on unhistoric acts; and that things are not so ill with you and me as they might have been, is half owing to the number who lived faithfully a hidden life, and rest in unvisited tombs."

India, 2006. This woman is from a tribal group of 2.5 million. I was told there were fewer than 100 Christians among them. She was not one of them. As I knelt before her, camera in position, I recall silently repeating to myself, "She is made in the image of God. In the image of God. She is made in the image of God."

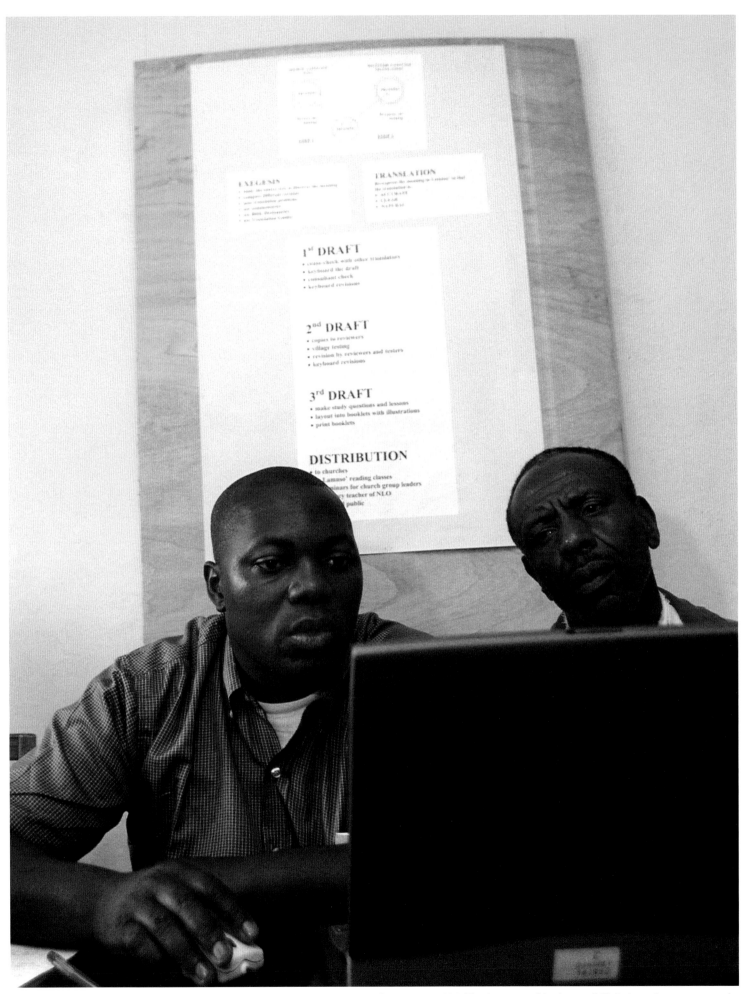

Cameroon, 2003. The legacy and heritage of Christian witness among the Nso people now bears witness to ongoing translation efforts—here, at an Old Testament workshop. These men are local church leaders, part of a team of 12 from four denominations working together.

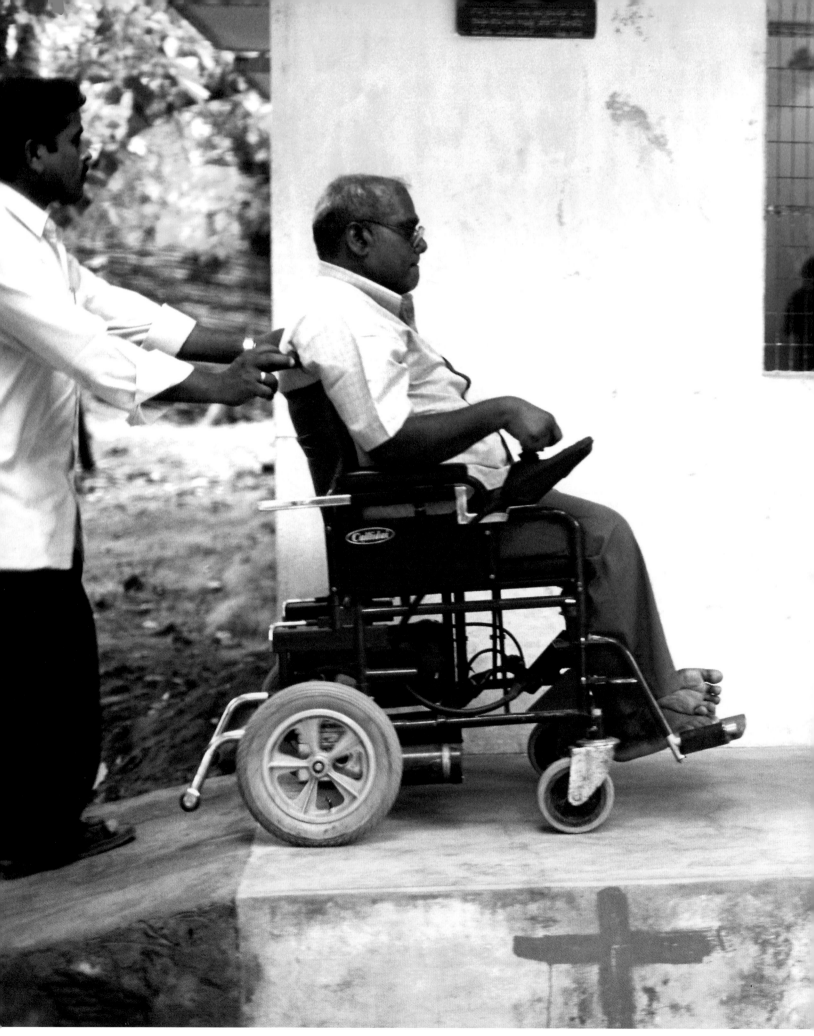

India, 2006. Handicapped by a stroke, veteran translator Devagnana-varam (Deva), is wheeled into a tiny Koya church—where the Koya New Testament he labored over is used. Deva suffered polio as a child. He also contracted tuberculosis. Later, while well into the translation project, his second son was born deaf and mute. Then a blood clot triggered the stroke that cripples him today. Depressed and unhealed, even though many prayed for him, he twice tried to commit suicide. Deva finally asked God to grant him enough life to complete the New

Testament. When I met him, he was conducting a workshop—training a Koya team to translate the Old Testament. For Deva, and others facing trials, there is encouragement in the hymn, Oh God Our Help In Ages Past, based on Psalm 90:

Time, like an ever rolling stream, bears all its sons away;
They fly, forgotten, as a dream dies at the opening day.
O God, our help in ages past, our hope for years to come;
Be thou our guide while life shall last, and our eternal home.

Partnership When 1 + 1 = 3

Cross-cultural math can be frustrating. Sometimes the differences between groups of people attempting to work together seem to cancel out any benefits of their endeavors. That is, until you do the math.

There is no potential like the potential born of synergism. The simultaneous actions of separate agencies or like-minded organizations and people, working together, can have a greater total effect than the sum of their individual efforts. That's when 1+1=3. And that addition is not bound by borders or cultures.

Nor is this kind of increase our own invention. As believers, we find it modeled in our foundational relationship with the ultimate partnership: God the Father, God the Son and God the Holy Spirit. While with us the whole can be greater than the sum of the parts, with God the whole *is* the sum of the parts.

For the family of Wycliffe organizations, partnership—*Vision 2025* style—includes two broad types of associations.

First, it involves substantial cooperation with the global Christian community in serving the Bibleless people groups of the earth. It is achieved by serving with local and national churches, individual Christians, Bible translation organizations, mission agencies, seminaries and Bible schools, funding agencies, etc.

Secondly, it embraces continuing alliances with our historic partners who share our concerns for linguistic minority groups. These alliances include local communities and their institutions, governmental agencies, educational organizations, non-governmental organizations (NGOs), and international multi-lateral organizations such as UNESCO.

The bottom line of partnership is the mutual empowerment to serve the Lord and one another in previously unimaginable ways. The true motivation for building and maintaining these partnerships is revealed in the faces of the people we serve—and in the ongoing challenge of bringing honor to God by working out how to work together.

Do nothing out of selfish ambition or vain conceit, but in humility consider others better than yourselves. Each of you should look not only to your own interests, but also to the interests of others.

—Philippians 2:3-4 (NIV)

Singapore, 2001. Kenneth Kok, of Wycliffe Singapore, and a first-generation Christian, has been instrumental in mobilizing churches in that region of southeast Asia to serve Bibleless groups. He's a champion for marginalized people. He's a partner.

Northwest Territories, Canada, 2002. Here's a team only God could put together. Swiss-born priest Father Jean Pochat (foreground) laughs it up with Wycliffe members Morina and Jaap Feenstra. Morina is from Malaysia; Jaap is Dutch. What do they have in common? Love and respect for the Dogrib people they all serve. Even though I spent only a short time with them, I'd say that same kind of love and respect was mutually shared among all three as well. You can't write that into a partnership contract.

British Columbia, Canada, 2002. After speaking at a missions conference at Burnaby Alliance Church, Wycliffe leader Dr. Peter Wang (right) talks with a young man who was in attendance. *Vision 2025* is not just a vision for Wycliffe. "This is a vision for the Church," notes Peter. "The important thing is that God is working . . . and we're going to be partners with whomever He has brought together."

Alaska, U.S.A., 1991. Dave Shinen chats with a Yupik hunter on St. Lawrence Island in the Bering Sea. Siberia, where half of the Yupik people live, lies across the sea, 38 miles away. For several years during the Bible translation project, Dave and his wife Mitzi responded to a request by the University of Alaska's linguistics department to develop Yupik textbooks and reading materials—along with training Yupik language instructors. That's a cooperative venture with a direct purpose and added benefit of encouraging the local community to value the overall translation goals.

Central Asia, 1999. This is what a multi-agency, multi-cultural team looks like, discussing the readability of freshly translated Scripture passages for a language group of nearly three million speakers. The scene represents the nitty-gritty of working together in the translation process. Not one of these individuals will likely receive any credit when the results of their years of work is finally published—at least not in this lifetime.

Cameroon, 1994. Pastor Bapile, co-translator of the Koonzime New Testament, stands before a grouping of the Koonzime Translation and Literacy Committee in a remote region of southeastern Cameroon. Sometimes, it *does* take a village.

British Columbia, Canada, 2002. Various educational and training institutions are part of the Wycliffe family of organizations. In such institutions, a successful collaboration between an administration and its board of directors is crucial to providing the environment necessary to equip students. Here, the president of the Canada Institute of Linguistics (CanIL), Dr. Mike Walrod (in sweater), walks to a restaurant in Burnaby with Bill Lim, chair of the CanIL board, along with others from the school. After enjoying some fabulous Chinese food, I was once again convinced that it's often the little things, like sharing a meal, that bond relationships extending into larger, mutually shared objectives—like pursuing the goals of *Vision 2025*.

Thailand, 2001. Doug Inglis (wearing tie) lectures at Payap University in Chiang Mai. His specialty is semantics, the study of word meanings—getting at the full connotation of a word in a given context. Pictured with Doug are three graduate students. It will be motivated national colleagues like these three who will increasingly oversee language projects in the surrounding region. This student/teacher relationship models a healthy connotation of the meaning of partnership—and of friendship.

Cameroon, 1993. Dr. Joseph Mfonyam is a translator and linguistic consultant, as well as a Wycliffe United Kingdom member. He's also highly respected, especially around his home area of Bafut in northwest Cameroon. When I visited him and his family there, he took fresh printouts of Bafut Scripture he had been translating to the daily 5 a.m. Bible study at his church. There he could immediately gauge its impact among his neighbors and fellow believers. This picture was taken after one of those early gatherings, back at his home, as the morning light broke through cloud cover. To me, it was the Son warming his face.

Thailand, 2001. Of the 170 residents of this Lahu village in northern Thailand, 130 are Christian. Already, young adults—who, like these children, grew up in this area—are serving as cross-cultural missionaries with Wycliffe Thailand.

Cameroon, 1994. Covered by the shade of a flame tree, Wycliffe member Patricia Wilkendorf and Pastor Jean-Jules Biondokin review a draft of the book of Hebrews he has translated into his Nomaande language.

Cambodia, 2001. Yeh Paduu, a mother tongue translator, works full time for a consortium of five partner agencies called International Co-operation for Cambodia—a registered NGO serving ethnic groups in Cambodia.

Peru, 2005. Novelist James Baldwin wrote: "Not everything that is faced can be changed, but nothing can be changed until it is faced." A Quechua child stands in the doorway of a small village church. Inside, his parents are among many attending a seminar aimed at healing marriages—where all the material presented is in the Cusco Quechua language. Wycliffe members support and train Quechua writers who, in turn, produce such vernacular literacy materials. The writers are part of the Christian organization in Peru known as ATEK, which in English stands for "The association that shines the gospel to the Quechua-speaking world."

Mali, 2004. According to Malian Pastor Nouh Ag Infa Yattara, "In Africa, no child is abandoned." Certainly not here in Timbuktu. Pastor Nouh related this to me while checking in on his small, church-run center for orphans called Elijah House. He is *the* focal point of Christian partnership between numerous agencies—including Wycliffe—and churches in the fabled, predominately Muslim town on the edge of the Sahara Desert. He also initiated the now completed New Testament translation into his Tamasheq language.

Central Asia, 1999. Isaak (right), his wife and two children share a meal at the invitation of friends (seated at left). As a South Korean member of a Wycliffe partnering agency, Isaak's awareness of Asian values is a key reason why he and his family have integrated so well here as translation advisors for a major language group.

India, 2006. An entire Gadaba village in Orissa state listens to a draft of Luke 15 in their language for the first time. Varghese John (holding text, center) seeks their input, because he's not a native Gadaba speaker. Varghese, a translator with the Wycliffe organization in India, Word For All, is from an entirely different area in southern India. It was a long process for the Gadaba people to accept him and his family into the village. They were initially only able to find a cow shed to live in.

In Luke 15, Jesus tells the parable of the lost sheep. Since the Gadaba are but a small language group within India's billion-plus population, I wonder if the keen interest the villagers showed that evening stemmed from hearing Jesus say, "Suppose one of you had a hundred sheep and lost one. Wouldn't you leave the ninety-nine . . . and go after the lost one until you found it?" (*The Message*).

Capacity Building
It's A People Process

"Even though a bird flies, his bones end up in the ground."—Tamasheq proverb

This saying by the nomads of the Sahara Desert could have several meanings, depending on the context. But it surely reflects the transitory nature of our trajectories in this life. Our plans (even organizationally) may fly high for a time, propelled by our own enthusiasm, skill sets and sometimes just adrenaline. But gravity and time will inevitably ground such plans if we fail to engage with others in a meaningful way.

Capacity building is a two-way street. Its reciprocal nature describes an exchange process between caring and capable people of different cultures. For the Wycliffe family of organizations, this process involves developing the necessary skills, infrastructure and network of relationships essential to language development and Bible translation programs.

Results emerge: trained personnel, sufficient funding, and individuals as well as institutions that can provide the guidance and consultation vital to fulfilling *Vision 2025*, and even moving beyond that vision.

Sometimes, building up colleagues and partners committed to Bible translation in their own language communities means first breaking down one's own misconceptions—often naively or innocently held—about what others need and want for themselves. That's why capacity building is a people process. All those involved in achieving common goals like *Vision 2025* must be learners—from each other, and from our mutual source, our Father in Heaven.

As author John Andrew Holmes put it: "It is well to remember that the entire universe, with one trifling exception, is composed of others."

Therefore encourage one another and build each other up, just as in fact you are doing.
—1 Thessalonians 5:11 (NIV)

Peru, 2005.

Cambodia, 2001. A group of more than 20 men attend a writer's workshop to compose literacy materials in their own Krung language in a remote village in Ratanakiri province. These are some of the first such indigenous language curricula developed in the country.

Peru, 2005. Quechua pastor Luis Cervantes came to Lima from his home in the highlands of southern Peru to study at the International Course of Linguistics, Translation and Literacy. These classes, held in Spanish, provide first-rate linguistic training and are part of the growing worldwide effort by Wycliffe and partners to make such training available in local contexts. Luis is helping adapt an existing Scripture translation in a related dialect for the 260,000 of his people who speak the Eastern Apurimac dialect of Quechua.

Cameroon, 2003. For nearly a decade, Moise Yonta (right) and Wycliffe translation consultant Karl Grebe spent countless hours working together on a Bible translation and literacy project for the Ngiemboon people. With the knowledge and experience he gained, Moise now helps oversee many translation programs as a leader in the partner organization, Cameroon Association for Bible Translation and Literacy.

Cameroon, 1995. These Bakossi women are seeing an alphabet chart in their language for the first time. Their smiles express a budding awareness of what is now possible for them.

Peru, 2005. Literacy specialist Justin Hettinga chats with a Quechua man atop a misty 14,000-foot pass. Justin is part of a team organizing literacy training workshops, among other programs, with two indigenous Quechua organizations in Peru devoted to helping their own communities develop in reading and applying translated Scripture. Justin and his non-Peruvian Wycliffe colleagues intentionally plan to leave Peru by 2010. Their daily passion: to come alongside and help Quechua Christian organizations and church leaders realize their own goals and vision.

Cambodia, 2001. Among other benefits, literacy helps instill value in people and how they operate in the society around them. These children, in rural northeast Cambodia, not far from parts of the old Ho Chi Minh Trail, wait until evening for their mother tongue reading classes to begin—that is when their teachers are available after tending their crops.

Peru. 2005. As part of the literacy team working with two Quechua organizations (see caption, pg. 67), Carletta Roche enjoys a moment with children of potato farmer Albino Mamani at their home near the town of Patacancha. Albino teaches and supervises several local literacy classes in his Cusco Quechua language. His children are literally beginning their learning in their own backyard.

West Asia, 1997. These women are learning to read by using a primer in their own language—a sight that is not nearly common enough among women of marginalized people groups around the world. Unaccustomed to, yet apparently unafraid of, a foreign photographer sitting amongst them, they carried on with focused intent.

Cameroon, 2003. How do you spell 'intrinsic worth'?
By using your own alphabet.

Bolivia, 2005. At the Evangelical Mennonite Church in Pailón, Bolivia, children of families who are outcast from nearby conservative Mennonite colonies attend a Sunday school class in their modest facility. The class is conducted in their Plautdietsch mother tongue—and based on their Plautdietsch Bible.

Cameroon, 1994. A Babungo elder holds up his copy of the Babungo New Testament at a dedication ceremony. Increasingly, Wycliffe and partners work hard to provide vernacular Scripture in whatever medium is most suitable for different language communities. Our endeavors are not simply about *a* book. They're about *the* book.

Cameroon, 1994. I had just photographed the elder holding his New Testament (**opposite**) when I turned directly around and caught a glimpse of children watching, holding hands, as is common in African and many other cultures around the world. It occurred to me that each of these photographs represents different expressions of an outreach of love.

Mali, 2004. Key translator of the Tamasheq New Testament he's holding, Pastor Ibrahim Ag Mohamed awaits his time slot at a small radio station in the ancient city of Gao. Beaten as a child for speaking his own language, he now reads and teaches from the Tamasheq Scriptures to thousands of nomadic Tamasheq. On my visits to various people groups, I've often observed how a few key individuals can so powerfully influence their communities. Sometimes capacity building is simply about connecting with and equipping those key people—like Pastor Ibrahim—who have already been gifted by God.

Cambodia, 2001. Wycliffe members and ethnomusicologists, Mary and Todd Saurman, conduct a workshop in northeast Cambodia to develop indigenous music. Todd (in background) notes, "It is especially rewarding to communicate how valuable they, their language, and their music are to God."

Thailand, 2001. Doug Inglis, center background (see pg. 49), joins a group of mother tongue translators as they check and polish a translation of the Book of Proverbs. One of Doug's roles has been to serve as a trainer at workshops, fostering sessions like this one in northern Thailand, where participants come from the surrounding region.

What's missing from this picture? Nothing—it's what capacity building looks like.

In times past in regions of the Middle East, goatskins were fashioned into wine containers. As the grape juice initially poured in became fermented, both the liquid and the skin would expand. But if the juice was poured into an already stretched and used skin, the natural expansion process would crack the old wineskin, draining away the contents.

In terms of *Vision 2025*, the theme of creative strategies is all about seeking new ways for the translation and use of God's Word to increase (harmoniously within the language communities it's meant for) using practices or processes not subject to failure because they are outdated or mismatched.

In the big picture of accomplishing *Vision 2025*, Wycliffe and its partners are embracing new attitudes, seeking to broaden our repertoire of strategies, and working differently to maximize our effectiveness. For example, new technologies are being created and tried, including the development of software, to speed translation work.

But employing creative initiatives does not mean abandoning tried and true principles, like maintaining translation standards. A case in point: it is both creative and effective to pour time and resources into preparing Bible translation exegetical reference texts—often available only in English—for numerous national languages, so that mother tongue translators can easily use them. It's like laying down both rails on a railroad track, enabling the train to move resolutely forward.

Inevitably, there are failures that come with trying to implement new ideas. Leaders in Wycliffe and partnering organizations know this all too well. These seeming setbacks call for times of reflection, which can lead to even better strategies.

There is a quote attributed to Wayne Gretzky, arguably the greatest hockey player of all time, and noted for his uncanny ability to "see" and anticipate all that was unfolding before him on the ice: "You miss 100% of the shots you don't try." By continually taking a fresh approach, aiming to see and anticipate what needs to be done, we stretch, grow, are filled—and are poured out for His purposes.

Neither do men pour new wine into old wineskins. If they do, the skins will burst, the wine will run out and the wineskins will be ruined. No, they pour new wine into new wineskins and both are preserved.

—Matthew 9:17 (NIV)

Dallas, U.S.A., 2002. An example of specialized font design developed to aid in research and translation projects. SIL, Wycliffe's key partner organization, has teams of highly creative staff in several locations around the world devoted to inventing beautiful and precise digital forms of writing used for publishing translated Scripture.

West Asia, 1997. Snake charmers in this area belong to the lowest caste in the society around them. It's difficult to look up when other people always look down on you. For many in this area of the world, regional socio-economic issues, as well as linguistic and even security matters, are just some of the factors which make people like these some of the hardest to reach with Bible translation. It becomes imperative to engage and equip the growing Church in the global South and East to embrace translation efforts in their local contexts.

Caucasus region, southeastern Europe, 1999. Object of friendly discussion in a village square, a language surveyor (foreground, right) plies his trade. He's using sentence repetition tests and questionnaires to help determine a variety of language-related needs, including Bible translation. Several years after this survey trip, a translation project was indeed launched for this people group.

Northwest Territories, Canada, 2002. Wycliffe team members working in the Dogrib New Testament translation project acknowledge John B. Zoe (pictured), a forward-looking young Dogrib leader, as the catalyst in facilitating mother tongue speakers to do the translation. John, the Dogrib's chief land-claims negotiator with the federal government, became the chairman of the translation committee, and is the embodiment of good strategy: that is, working with a good (and influential) friend.

Peru, 2005. In all my years photographing vernacular literacy classes, it was rare to see such giggling. Here's why these women were laughing: as part of introducing often illiterate Quechua to reading, a series of booklets integrating biblical principles have been produced, which address common social problems in their culture. Here, a Quechua literacy worker reads to women for the first time in their language from a booklet about family violence. They're laughing not because the issue is funny, but because they identify with the abusive language used by the husband in the story. The idea is to make the Bible practical—presenting concepts that can impact their lives.

Papua New Guinea, 1990. "We see and hear it. Now we understand." —PNG villager. For many language groups, the printed word is not a foundation of their cultures. Thus, using all sorts of non-print media in translation projects (including, for example, the *JESUS* film) is an increasing strategy within *Vision 2025*.

Cameroon, 2003. At a workshop for Old Testament translators, a team member uses *Paratext*, software developed by the United Bible Societies. He's comparing his Nso language translation of verses in Genesis 4 with several English versions and the original Hebrew, right on his computer screen.

Mali, 2004. SIDA, in French, is the acronym for AIDS. The rest of this public awareness billboard in the town of Djenné needs no further translation. Wycliffe staff and partnering agencies have developed mother tongue AIDS publications for dozens of minority people groups around the world. These help break down societal taboos hindering community discussion about AIDS—simply because the materials are in their own languages.

Forget the former things;
do not dwell on the past.
See I am doing a new thing!
Now it springs up;
do you not perceive it?
I am making a way in the desert
and streams in the wasteland.
The wild animals honor me,
the jackals and the owls,
because I provide water
in the desert and
streams in the wasteland,
to give drink to my people,
my chosen,
the people I formed for myself
that they may proclaim
my praise.
Isaiah 43:18-21

Kenya, 1997. Wycliffe translator Loren Koehler climbs the stairwell leading to his family's apartment in Nairobi. The Koehler family, along with many other language teams, were displaced from their work, because of civil unrest in former Zaire, now the Democratic Republic of Congo. They all face the challenge of figuring out ways to continue their work, and are reminded daily by the Scripture wall hanging of how God views their situation.

Washington, D.C., U.S.A., 1999. SIL, Wycliffe's key partner dedicated to training, language research, translation and literacy, maintains an office in Washington, D.C. Leaders and future leaders from around the world come here as ambassadors for their countries. Also, headquartered here are many multi-lateral agencies who have influence affecting minority language communities. Alan MacDonald, director of the SIL team in D.C., heads across the lobby of the World Bank headquarters to a meeting with officials there.

Papua New Guinea, 1989. A tiny village perched on a sub-ridge of the massive Sarawaget Range in Morobe province illustrates the geographical barriers that have helped shape more than 800 languages in Papua New Guinea. Many Wycliffe staff have worked in PNG over the years, which in time has led to the "exportation" of much invaluable experience to new areas of service—including training of national colleagues and translation consultants.

West Asia, 1997. When asked of his motivation for a particular sculpture, Michelangelo replied, "I saw an angel in the stone, and carved to set it free." In areas of the world where there are opposing forces to Bible translation, a comparable vision and creativity must be employed. Engaging local church networks is vital to realizing the ultimate goal of lives transformed by God's Word.

Papua New Guinea, 1990. "Even the birds are jealous" (Bumper sticker inside a missionary aircraft). The geographic isolation of this country's language groups (see caption, pg. 93) has meant the extensive use of mission aviation as a key strategy—due in large part to the over 50 year relationship with JAARS, Wycliffe's partner organization specializing in aviation and other technologies and services in support of the Bible translation movement.

Peru, 2005. Using vernacular electronic media in remote villages with no electricity means these Quechua Scripture promoters must bring their power with them. But learning to use flexible solar panels to charge portable batteries is only part of a larger training program that these men have participated in, provided by Wycliffe staff serving as vernacular media specialists.

Bolivia, 2005. Children living in Old Colony Mennonite communities intentionally receive only basic schooling in the belief that anything more leads to "worldliness." But these children, from families who've left conservative colonies, are now receiving education as part of the ministry of the Evangelical Mennonite Church in Pailón, where they use the Bible translated into their Plautdietsch mother tongue. (See caption, pg. 73.) Wycliffe personnel were involved in the translation of *De Bibel,* and its usage is a key aid for other Mennonites ministering to the colony families.

Washington, D.C., U.S.A., 1999. Just another day at the office. Alan MacDonald (see caption, pg. 91) and colleague Ron Gluck, right, pay a visit to an ambassador. It's a visit that can ultimately give birth to relationships—on earth and for eternity.

Sustainability
The Art of Transition

John the Baptist had a successful ministry and a large following when Jesus entered the scene. When John's disciples informed him that many were leaving him to follow Jesus, John recognized that his purpose was fulfilled. And he was glad: " . . . the friend of the bridegroom, who stands and hears him, rejoices greatly because of the bridegroom's voice. Therefore this joy of mine is fulfilled. He must increase, but I *must* decrease" (John 3:29, 30 NKJV).

Increase and decrease denote a process, not an immediate takeover and withdrawal. The staff of Wycliffe organizations and partnering agencies is committed to seeing that what has been started in language development and Bible translation will be brought as close to a point of sustainability as possible, given local and national conditions. As we phase out of our roles in any given language project, it should be possible for local and national leadership to continue translation and other language activity according to their available resources. We desire to see our mutual efforts bear long-term fruit, even in our eventual absence. Thus we invest in people, and the processes by which they can, in time, maintain their language and translation programs.

The key point of this aspect of *Vision 2025* is the sliding scale of knowing how to transition from daily hands-on involvement, to applying a progressively lighter touch. Ultimately, our role is to use our cumulative skills, training and resources to establish a foundation, and then *get out of the way*, corporately speaking.

It's easier to get out of the way for others to carry on the work when we remember that God is the ultimate sustainer. For both individuals and the Wycliffe family of organizations, it is He who has brought us to this point. It is He who has kept and preserved us to accomplish His work. He will take others on from here.

The Son is the radiance of God's glory and the exact representation of his being, sustaining all things by his powerful word.
—Hebrews 1:3a (NIV)

Mali, 2004. " . . . he [Jesus] sent them out two by two" (Mark 6:7a NIV). Pastors Nouh (left) and Ibrahim—chief driving forces behind the translation and publication of the Tamasheq New Testament—walk the dusty streets of the fabled city of Timbuktu. Love is the most enduring factor of Christian witness.

Mali, 2004. Wycliffe member Marko Hakkola speaks with men from the Bozo language group outside a mosque, as it's an opportunity to practice his language learning. Marko noted that, "You're making yourself dependent. . . . You say, 'I'm like a child. I need your help.'" The startup of so many translation projects begins with being humble. The long-term viability of such projects requires remaining that way.

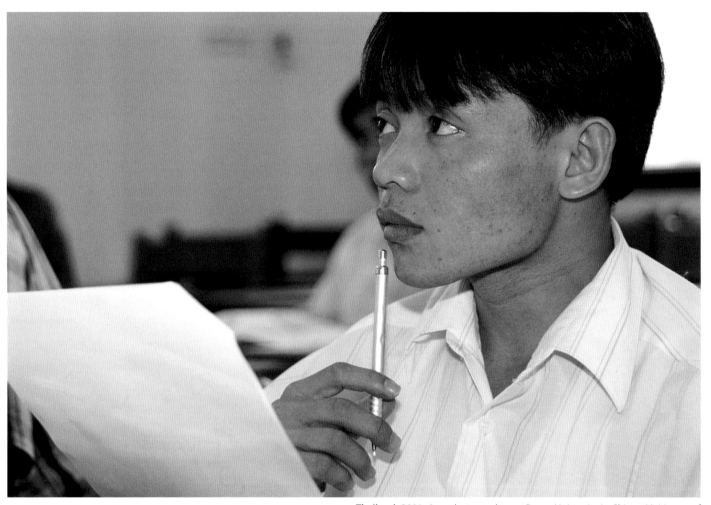

Thailand, 2001. A graduate student at Payap University in Chiang Mai is one of many representing a variety of language groups in Southeast Asia. They attend high-level linguistic courses in preparation for leading language development and translation work back in their home communities.

India, 2006.

For millions in South Asia who are without God's Word in their own language, the following questions are heart-rending: "But how can they call on him to save them unless they believe in him? And how can they believe in him if they have never heard . . .

. . . faith comes from hearing, that is, hearing the Good News about Christ" (Romans 10:14a, 17 NLT). For this young Quechua girl in southern Peru, helping to lead worship among her people comes naturally. The entire Bible is now available in her language, and it continues to nourish and sustain believers in the Church there.

Peru, 2005.

Kenya, 1997. Boys sit in a Sunday school class that's part of the ministry of a large Nairobi church. African churches are numerous and growing across the continent, and will continue to be key resources for sustaining ongoing translation programs.

India, 2006. Hard work in any language, Part I—linguistic training, that is. These students form part of the vanguard of young Indians uniquely called to serve among India's 180 language groups with no Scripture. Most seek long-term ministry. All seek God's sustaining grace.

Central Asia, 1999. Hard work in any language, Part II—field work, that is. A mother tongue translator (left) and a Wycliffe colleague, whose specialty is to advise on original Greek meanings of biblical texts, grapple with a concept in a translated passage from the book of Galatians. Getting God's Word right is never wrong. But it can take awhile.

India, 2006. sus·tain (sə stān'): to provide for the support of; to carry the burden of; to comfort; to encourage; to uphold the validity of; to keep in existence.

Peru, 2005. At a small rural church in the village of Huano-quite, this Quechua couple is attending a marriage seminar—all part of gradually putting Scripture use efforts into the hands of leaders in the Quechua Church of southern Peru. They have just finished an exercise in which each spouse pins a note on the other's sweater identifying "weeds" in their marriage, such as insults, criticism and anger. They then pin a second note that lists the "good seeds" they intend to plant: patience, understanding and love.

Quebec, Canada, 2001. A privilege our family has occasionally had together over the years has been to witness Scripture dedication events. At Lake Mistissini, on the morning of the James Bay Cree New Testament dedication, a symbolic "walking out" ceremony took place, involving the local children. Here is my daughter Meredith's description of the ceremony, written at age 11: *"When we arrived at the walkout ceremony, it was drizzling, but that didn't matter to the Cree people that morning. Aided by a guardian (a parent or grand-* *parent), the children who were just learning to walk stepped out of the teepee. Just as the children were walking out into the world, the New Testament in the James Bay Cree language was presented to the community as a good and wonderful thing. This is what I enjoyed most that day: seeing the children being guided by their guardians into the world, in harmony with the fact that the Cree people will receive guidance from the Word of God throughout their lives."*

Cameroon, 2003 (above and opposite right); **Alberta, Canada, 2003** (opposite far right). Organizations, mission agencies, churches—they all consist of people like you and me. Sometimes, even in the course of providing God's Word to others, God's people suffer incredible trials and loss. Wycliffe missionaries David and Henny Thormoset, above, felt such loss when their son Andreas took his own life in 2001. He had been living with relatives back home in Canada while the rest of the family was in Cameroon. It was only God's all-sufficient grace that sustained Henny and her family. (**Opposite**) Reproduced with her blessing is an excerpt from her diary, written shortly after Andreas was buried.

Here I am now, for the first time in my life, not being able to get what I want more than anything else. I want the past three weeks to be undone. I want my son. I want to undo history and to have a second chance. I want it desperately, and God's answer is a resounding NO. It is final. I have no second chance. I can throw a fit or pray 'till I am blue in the face. But I cannot and will not ever get this thing that I so desperately want. Now I am put to the test. Can I say that, yes, God, you are good, all the time?

Yes, God, you are good. I know it. I believe it. You are good, even though this spoiled child cannot have what she wants. You are good, because you have provided everything we need for salvation, for our best, for our eternal future. You are good because you forgive us for all our sins, including our failures to be perfect parents.

You are good because you give us what we don't deserve—grace and mercy. You are good because you never leave me; you give me peace and comfort in my darkest hour. You are good because you give me hope, the certainty of resurrection, both Andreas' resurrection and mine.

You are good because your love is constant, unconditional; not petty like mine. God, I declare that you are good to me. You are good to Andreas. He is safe. You took care of him by bringing him safely into your Kingdom. You rescued him from hell. You saved him. Thank you God. You have kept your promises to me. You took care of my son, when I was out of the picture, not able to control the situation. . . . I praise you God. You are a good God. I love you.

—Henny Thormoset

Cambodia, 2001. Children in Ratanakiri Province, northeast Cambodia.

Washington, D.C., USA, 1999. At the World Bank headquarters, participants at a video conference linking several African countries listen to Dr. Steve Walter (left), international literacy coordinator for SIL, Wycliffe's key partner organization devoted to language development. He's been invited to give an overview of what SIL has learned over the past half-century in the area of vernacular literacy in local language communities worldwide—like the SIL literacy program in the mother tongue of the children pictured **opposite**.

Thailand, 2001. Sustainable Bible translation programs refers to the presence of local, national or regional institutions that will help service the continuing needs of language communities. Translation: "The seed that fell on good soil represents those who truly hear and understand God's word and produce a harvest of thirty, sixty, or even a hundred times as much as had been planted!" (Matthew 13:23 NLT).

Beneath the Canopy
The Waorani of Ecuador

I n 1956 a small group of Ecuadorian Indians drew international attention when they speared and killed five missionaries who were attempting to establish contact with them. For many years, these Indians had been viewed as savages, or "Aucas," as outsiders called them. No one had succeeded in determining how they lived, what they believed or what they felt. No one even knew what they called themselves.

However, in 1958, Elisabeth Elliot and Wycliffe's Rachel Saint (wife of Jim Elliot, and sister of Nate Saint, respectively—two of the five missionaries killed) did succeed in peacefully contacting these people, who call themselves Waorani. The two women initiated the process of developing mutual understanding between the Waorani and the outside world. Slowly the Waorani began to lose their fear, distrust and hatred of outsiders, whom they had always called "cowodi," their word for savages.

Insight into the Waorani's existence revealed a people with a remarkable ability to survive, even thrive, in a harsh, demanding environment. Their technology at that time was limited to stone, wood and fiber. Their language has no words for "government" or "leader" because their culture has no formally organized groups. In addition, violent confrontations between rival Waorani factions, as well as with outsiders, were commonplace, and often ended in death. In fact, before 1958, one out of every two adult men among this group—whose entire population numbered roughly 500 at the time—died from being speared.

From the time that Elisabeth and Rachel made contact with the Waorani, and communicated to them an understanding of God's forgiveness, the Waorani's lives were fundamentally transformed. They were pierced in a new way—a way that ultimately led to the end of revenge killings. They turned away from a consuming fear and a drive for vengeance, toward believing in and following God. Their story spans the 20th and 21st centuries, as well as missionary generations, and it portrays the struggles and growth that any Christian community experiences.

A glimpse into Waorani life is represented on the following pages.

A girl climbs for papayas near the village of Tewaeno, in the rainforest of eastern Ecuador. All photographs in this photo essay are from Tewaeno and surrounding area, April, 1987

The Waorani are exceptionally skilled at living off the rainforest. They are remarkably healthy because of their high protein and carbohydrate diet and constant strenuous exercise. Kinta (above) carries his nine-foot-long blowgun, commonly used with poison tipped darts. It takes strength and precision to aim at monkeys and birds that are moving 100 feet up in the forest canopy.

During an all-day trip to a favorite fishing site, Waorani men shot, but only grazed, this capuchin monkey. It hid high up in the crook of a tree. The men chopped down the tree and ran the monkey down as it scampered over slippery, steep jungle terrain. They then tied a vine around its neck to carry it—to be part of that evening's meal. After arrival at the river, I sat down, exhausted. But the hunters barely paused to drop the monkey a few feet from me as they rushed out in pursuit of a pack of raccoon-like coatimundis. To my amazement, the not-yet-dead creature proceeded to untie the vine collar and make its es-

Close contact with jungle animals taken as pets teaches children from a young age about the habits, cries and smells of game animals. By the time this boy is old enough to hunt, he may know by a call or a scent in the leaves whether an animal high in the trees is one to be pursued, or a non-game species too small to bother with. Because this pet peccary's emerging tusks pose some danger, its fate as part of the village food supply is a possibility, although pets are usually released

(Opposite) A young girl plays in the Tewaeno River. **(Above)** Besides using spears to fish, as seen here, the Waorani also use a plant poison, or in larger rivers, dynamite. But the jungle is home to many dangers. Fresh water stingrays can inflict painful wounds. Jaguars inhabit the area. And the Waorani have one of the highest recorded mortality rates of any group anywhere due to poisonous snakebites.

Visitors from another village sparked a time of dancing
and singing. Fifty years ago a "visit" by another group of
Waorani could well have meant a surprise spearing raid.

(Opposite) Born around 1920 on a remote tributary of the Amazon, Geketa grew up knowing that to meet anyone from the outside world meant confrontation and death. Revered as a storyteller, his words remind the Waorani about their past. As part of that past, Geketa and Dewey (see pgs. 134, 135) were among the group of Waorani who killed the five missionaries in 1956. (Above) One of those five men was Nate Saint, brother of Rachel Saint, seen here among the people she loved. Geketa and Rachel (both now passed away) could not have come from more different backgrounds. Both had a profound impact on the Waorani for good. Geketa's influence was a key factor in the Waorani ending their devastating revenge killing cycles, and Rachel began translation work. The New Testament was dedicated in 1992. The translation team included Dr. Catherine Peeke, Rosi Jung, Dayuma Quento, Ino Enqueri, Ana Yeti, Ayiba Tani, Tementa Nenquihui, Oba Quento and others. Additionally, Pat Kelley was instrumental in developing a literacy program.

(Above) All 40 of Tewaeno's inhabitants attended this Easter morning church service
Dewey, speaking in front **(and opposite)**, has an unwavering commitment to main
taining peace, and is a strong factor of stability among the Waorani community. He
later held a Bible story time with the children, followed by soccer and volleyball

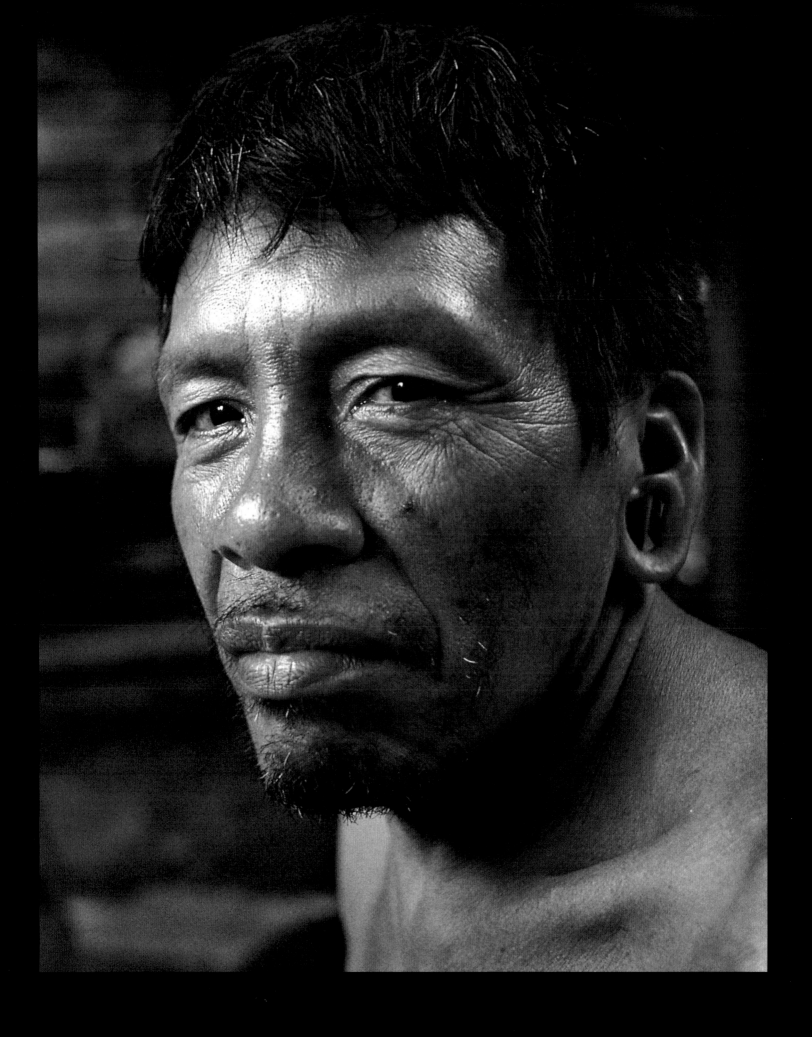

Represented here is the first generation of Waorani who have not been part of the revenge spearing cycles of the past. They are faced with the challenge of interacting with surrounding cultures. The Waorani's traditional homeland, once some 8,000 square miles, has been drastically reduced. Christianity's impact on a minority people group does not mean the removal of forces that make life difficult. But it does mean the introduction of a positive force—God's love and mercy—that is as unstoppable as the effect of a child's smile.

This sandbar on the Curaray River, known as Palm Beach, was the site of the 1956 spearing deaths of five men. That cataclysmic event impacted a generation of missionaries and others around the world, and its reverberations are still felt to this day. On January 8, 2006, it was the scene of a three-day memorial service marking the 50th anniversary of that event. As part of the service, 10 Waorani were baptized in the waters that once ran with the blood of their spiritual forefathers.

Prayer
Our Greatest Resource

What is prayer, but an ongoing conversation with God? In a conversation, sometimes we speak, sometimes we listen. Some of the best conversations are found in the silence, when we stop thinking of what to say, and "hear" with our eyes and our hearts. As it is written,

"The heavens declare the glory of God;
the skies proclaim the work of his hands.
Day after day they pour forth speech;
night after night they display knowledge.

There is no speech or language
where their voice is not heard.
Their voice goes out into all the earth,
their words to the ends of the world"
(Psalm 19:1-4 NIV).

Northwest Territories, Canada, 2003.

God is calling out to the people of the whole world, in every voice that might be heard, including His Word, in every language He created. He impresses us with the urgency of the task of Bible translation, so all can listen in a language that speaks to the heart. He encourages us to partner with others who are like-minded. He builds capacity in us to do the work. His are the most creative strategies. And He sustains us each step of the way, reminding us that with Him, nothing is impossible.

When we pray, when we listen, when we wait on the Lord, our strength is renewed. Prayer is our greatest resource because it connects us with the main source of all things, Jesus Christ—the Light of the World. He hears us, and knows us, on a level as deep as the heavens are high above us. And He taught His followers to pray to our Father in heaven (Matthew 6:9-13 NKJV), a prayer displayed above the photographs in this section.

Just as the Northern Lights are a phenomenon resulting from interaction of the sun with Earth's atmosphere, our interaction with the Light of the World gives us a vision of the very nature of God. He is the light that "shines in the darkness, and the darkness can never extinguish it" (John 1:5 NLT).

Hallowed be Your name

... *the hidden person of the heart, with the incorruptible beauty*
of a gentle and quiet spirit ... is very precious in the sight of God.
—1 Peter 3:4 (NKJV)

Cameroon, 1993.

I remember the days of long ago; I meditate on all your works and consider what your hands have done.
—Psalm 143:5 (NIV)

East Asia, 1998.

. . . For the mountains shall depart and the hills be removed, But my kindness shall not depart from you, Nor shall my covenant of peace be removed. . . .
—Isaiah 54:10 (NKJV)

Central Asia, 1999.

West Asia, 1997.

I would have lost heart, unless I had believed
That I would see the goodness of the LORD
In the land of the living.
Wait on the LORD;
Be of good courage,
And He shall strengthen your heart. . . .

—Psalm 27:13,14 (NKJV)

Papua New Guinea, 1990.

Cameroon, 1994.

Be thou my vision, O Lord of my heart;
Naught be all else to me, save that thou art—
Thou my best thought by day or by night,
Waking or sleeping, Thy presence my light.

—from the hymn, Be Thou My Vision

Russia, 1999.

Peru, 2005.

Thailand, 2001.

. . . My mercy and justice are coming soon.
My salvation is on the way.
My strong arm will bring justice to the nations.
All distant lands will look to me
and wait in hope. . . .

—Isaiah 51:5 (NLT)

Mali, 2004.

Cameroon, 1993.

Could we with ink the ocean fill,
And were the skies of parchment made,
Were every stalk on earth a quill,
And every man a scribe by trade,
To write the love of God above,
Would drain the ocean dry.
Nor could the scroll contain the whole,
Though stretched from sky to sky.

—from the hymn, The Love of God

For I am convinced that neither death nor life, neither angels nor demons, neither the present nor the future, nor any powers, neither height nor depth,

India, 2006.

nor anything else in all creation, will be able to separate us from
the love of God that is in Christ Jesus our Lord.

—Romans 8:38-39 (NIV)

Acknowledgements

During the production of this book, it became abundantly clear that we had taken on a project well beyond what we had anticipated. At times we felt overwhelmed, our abilities taxed. However, the prompting to begin and the bursts of inspiration throughout the production process were a constant reminder from the Lord that He who spurred us to undertake the work would help us see it to completion. We are grateful to Him for that.

We appreciate our children, Jordan and Meredith, for their patience with us while we worked on the book—and for accompanying one or both of us on various trips, including a highly memorable visit to Timbuktu by Jordan and Dave.

We humbly acknowledge our families and ministry supporters who have prayed for us and stood by us so faithfully for nearly a quarter century.

We thank our colleagues at the Wycliffe Canada main office in Calgary—notably the communications department staff, and also the Executive Director, Dave Ohlson, for the encouragement and administrative backing to publish this book.

We also owe special gratitude to Al Neufeld and the team at the McCallum Printing Group in Edmonton for giving us such expert advice and for being true partners in ministry to those people groups without God's Word in their own language.

Finally, we thank the hundreds of our Wycliffe colleagues and partners working in a variety of cross-cultural settings, who have eased the way for us, making interaction with the people pictured in this book possible, and by extension, the photographs themselves.

And for the incredible privilege of relating to and photographing individuals from language groups around the world, words seem insufficient. We trust the images convey the integrity and grand design which our common Creator has composed.

About the Authors

Originally from California, with a background in film production, photography and writing, Deborah has been a missionary with Wycliffe Bible Translators, serving in media production, since 1984.

Having recently finished home schooling her two children for more than 12 years, she continued throughout those years to contribute articles for Wycliffe Canada's quarterly publication, *Word Alive*.

Previously, Deborah has been a part of the production staff on two other Wycliffe books, *The Alphabet Makers* and *Any Given Day in the Life of the Bible*.

Prior to joining Wycliffe with Deborah in 1984, Dave was an instructor with Outward Bound, and then taught in the areas of film and multimedia production at a community college in California.

Dave earned his MS degree in professional photography from Brooks Institute of Photography in Santa Barbara, California, and has taught photography workshops at Latigo Ranch in Colorado.

He currently serves as a photographer for and co-editor of *Word Alive* magazine, and directs the Wycliffe Canada communications department, located in Calgary, Alberta.

West Asia, 1997. It's not what you look at, but what you see.

India, 2006. This boy was a fellow traveler, stuck in a massive traffic jam in Hyderabad. It is the final frame of film I exposed before embarking on this book project—and the inspiration for the book's title.